The
Magic
of
Irish Nature

The Magic of Irish Nature

Patrick O'Sullivan

NONSUCH

First published 2008

Nonsuch Publishing
73 Lower Leeson Street
Dublin 2
Ireland
www.nonsuchireland.com

British Library Cataloguing in Publication Data.
A catalogue record for this book is available from the British Library.

ISBN 978 1 84588 936 4

Typesetting and origination by Nonsuch Publishing.

Illustrations by Michelle Russell.

Printed and bound in Great Britain by Athenaeum Press Ltd.

Dedicated to those who

believe in the magic.

Contents

Foreword

The late poet, philosopher and mystic John Moriarty once related to me how, when he had returned home from Canada having spent a long time there, he felt emotionally and spiritually un-housed. All his book knowledge had left him wanton. One morning he set off over the hills in north Kerry on his own. He came across a hare's form. Admiring the wild shape in the wild grasses, he lay down and stretched out, with his head sheltered inside the nest. As he lay there silently, staring at the clouds, listening to a skylark sing and hover above, he imagined the form working like a healing poultice on his brain. He fell asleep and when he awoke he felt so much stronger, with an easing of his mental state; he felt he had experienced the healing powers of wild nature.

We live in an age in which we believe we are somehow outside of nature, not part of it, ever ready to exploit all those natural resources. Of course we do our bit for the environment: we recycle our plastic bottles, papers, etc. – our own rubbish. This is in itself a very worthwhile thing but what of our true relationship with our earth, the blue planet, mother nature? The place that we are born into that we will be laid to rest in. The place that gives us all the things we need to survive as a species.

How did we damage that precious bond with our home planet? The more we are catapulted ever forward into our technological and vertical world, the more there is a gaping hole in our psyche that we yearn to fill with something real. Our ancient ancestors had a unique relationship with the natural world, believing that they were part of it, not separate from it, even imagining the earth to possess a soul and a spirit. We may dismiss such notions as fanciful, yet there is a strange sense of urgency about these times, about the future of our planet. It's not so much the planet that we need to be concerned about, but ourselves. If we insist on being an irritant to her, she will just shake us off.

We need to rediscover our relationship with our home planet – we need the re-enchantment of nature in our lives and our culture.

When nature reveals its beauty and majesty, we are rewarded with wonderful works of art – poetry, sculptures, photography and music, weavings, designs, etc., that talented people produce for our enjoyment and inspiration.

There is a story about the great composer Beethoven, who was found sitting quietly on a log in a forest in Vienna by two painters carrying their canvases and paints. They greeted him and were curious to know why he was sitting alone in the forest. 'Seeking inspiration', he replied. 'But you're a composer, should you not be sitting at your desk at home? We are artists that's why we are here', they argued. 'Well, you are not artists if you don't know why I'm here', Beethoven retorted. Later in life, when he realised he was going deaf, he wrote in his diary, 'Hope is falling away from me as the leaves from the trees.'

The Magic of Irish Nature is such a welcome addition to our bookshelves. It weaves such gems of myths, legends and folklore with nature itself, opening an enchanted doorway that the sensitive, the curious, the wise and the innocent may enter freely and be enriched by the spellbinding tales and healing powers, reminding us that the myths and the enchantment of nature have always been part of our great story.

Congratulations to Patrick O'Sullivan for his great efforts and for adding another important strand to help us connect with our mystic past and enchanted isles. A special word of praise to artist Michelle Russell for her liquid, almost shape-shifting illustrations, which add to the enjoyment of this collection.

I will leave the last words to the great poet Percy Bysshe Shelley:

I am the eye with which the Universe
Beholds itself, and knows itself Divine
                              'Hymn of Apollo'

Don Conroy

Nature and Creation

Empathy with nature is very much part of Irish myth. When Suibhne Geilt was driven mad by the horrors of battle, he left the place and went to live all alone in the wilderness. He loved the trees, he said, for whether they were bleak and bare, or close and sheltering, they were always his friends. He lived on the things of nature: water and watercress and the fruits of the forest. He numbered the birds amongst his companions too, 'Sweeter to me the voice of the cuckoo along the river than the sound of ringing bells.' His house was wild and so was like a garden without a fence around it, 'God from heaven, he is the thatcher who

has thatched it.' He loved all the sounds of nature: the fluted notes of the blackbird on the mountain; the cry of the red grouse heard at dawn; the belling of the stag in a storm, the herons of Cuailgne calling in summer.

In the same way, Goll, a young warrior of the Fianna, fled from the horrors of battle to Gleann na nGealt where he too lived on watercress and wild fruits. Another of Finn's troop wrote a poem for his beloved:

If I am to be grateful to the woman,
to Cred for whom the cuckoo sings
in songs of praise she will ever live,
if she repay me for my gift.

So wrote the handsome Cael and the image of the cuckoo was his way of telling Cred that she was as lovely as summer itself. Another verse describes a bowl full of the juices of berries 'with which she colours her eyebrows', one of the earliest references to cosmetics in Irish literature.

Aonghus was the son of the Dagda, the father of all the gods, and the goddess Boand. He was given in fosterage to the god Midir of Bri Leith. Later, when Aonghus had grown up and was in possession of the Bruig at New Grange, Midir came to visit him. It was during this visit that Midir was accidentally blinded in one eye when a sprig of holly was hurled at him. Amongst the compensations he sought was the hand of the fairest woman in Ireland, 'I know of a woman whose beauty excels that of every woman in Eriu. She is Etain Echraide, the daughter of King Ailill of Ulster.' Aonghus then went to see Etain at the home of her father, but the latter was willing to part with her only on certain conditions, 'Twelve lands of mine that are nothing but waste and wild must be cleared so that men may dwell in them and that they may be suitable for games, assemblies and fortifications.' It was in fact Aonghus's father, the Dagda, who undertook the clearing of the twelve great plains but then Etain's father demanded something new – the diversion to the sea of twelve great rivers that were in springs in the bogs and marshes. In this way, not only would the land be drained, but his people too would enjoy the fruits of the sea.

Again it was the Dagda who caused the rivers to run to the sea in a single night. Each of the rivers and plains is mentioned by name in the ancient texts, every one representing the work of creation in its own way. 'Mag' was the old Irish word for a plain and so some of the plains were called Mag Lemna, Mag Tochair, Mag Mile, Mag Techt. Amongst the rivers were Findi, Slenae and Or. The naming of the rivers and plains illustrates the old Irish love of 'dindshenchas' or place lore. It was only when Etain's father was given her weight in silver and gold, however, that he finally agreed to part with her.

Accounts of the earliest invasions of Ireland, under the likes of Partholon and Nemed, also refer to the clearing of plains and the creation of rivers and lakes. Partholon, for instance, cleared four plains and Nemed twelve, while lakes magically burst forth from the earth when some sort of digging was going on. Very often this was the digging of a grave for some lately deceased member of the company, after whom the new lake was duly

named. The creation, naming and subsequent division of the land is very much part of the stuff of Irish myth. The most important river of course was the Boyne, which was sometimes described as 'the roof of the ocean'. It was named after the goddess Boand, the goddess of the white cow. In representing the different colours of cattle, it was said that she also symbolised the various phases of the moon. She followed the Boyne back to its source and was submerged in it, thus becoming its resident divinity. In the same way Sionnan, the daughter of Lodan, became submerged in the River Shannon and gave it her name.

The reigning monarch was very much identified with nature and the earth itself. The relation between a king and his realm was often portrayed

as a marriage, while his inauguration took on the
character of a wedding feast. The importance of
all things agricultural was illustrated time and
again. When Bres, son of Elatha was asked how
the men of Ireland should plough and sow and
reap, he replied, 'their ploughing shall be on a
Tuesday, their sowing the same, their reaping
the same again'. This was a magic formula which
recurred in later folk charms.

Different provinces were identified with
different aspects of nature. Munster, for instance,
was associated with honey bees, the latter having
a secret wisdom which they brought with them
from the Otherworld. When Midir brought the
beautiful Etain home to Bri Leith, his first wife
Fuamnach grew jealous of her and turned her
into a glorious scarlet fly:

> This fly was the size of the head of the most
> handsome man in Eriu and the music it made and
> the beating of its wings was sweeter than the music
> of pipes and harps and horns. Its eyes were like
> jewels in the dark and not only its colour but its
> fragrance too was enough to satisfy the hunger of
> any man. Even the smallest of drops that fell from
> its wings was a cure for sickness and disease.

Fuamnach then caused a magic wind which carried the fly across the sea. It was years and years later that the fly alighted on a rooftop in Ulster, then falling into the golden cup of one of the women of the place, namely the wife of Etar. The woman swallowed the fly and in this way was Etain reborn as the daughter of Etar.

Fish in Irish Myth

The Salmon of Knowledge, the 'bradán feasa', is perhaps the most celebrated fish in Irish mythology. The nine hazels of wisdom grew over the Well of Knowledge and when the nuts fell down they were eaten by the salmon below. Those who ate of the salmon were destined to become seers or poets or to have great gifts in some way.

When Finn Mac Cumhail, then called Demne, longed to learn poetry, he came to the druid Finnegas on the River Boyne. The druid had been watching for the Salmon of Knowledge for seven years, for it had been prophesied of him that he would taste of the salmon and thereafter nothing would be unknown to him. When the magic salmon was finally caught, Demne was asked to cook it, but given strict instructions that he was not to eat any of it. Demne, however noticed a blister on the side of the fish and accidentally burned his thumb on it, then putting his thumb in his mouth to soothe it. According to one version, he knew at once what was happening in the royal courts of Tara and Emhain Macha. 'Finn is your name', said the druid when the young Demne told him what had happened, 'For you was the Salmon of Knowledge given to be eaten.' He also told Finn to keep himself out of the way of the High King for a while, but that when the time came to acquaint the king with his newly acquired gift, whereupon he would make him leader of the Fianna, 'Thus was the knowledge given to Finn for whenever he put his thumb to his mouth, what ever he did not know was made known to him.' The chewing of the thumb also led to the tradition that Finn had a tooth of wisdom, 'det fis'. With his gift, Finn foretold many great events including the coming of the Danes and the emergence of Diarmuid MacMurrough.

There were other salmon in Irish tradition, however. *Lebor Gabála Érenn* gives a list of the various mythical invaders of Ireland. The very first invasion was led by a woman called Cessair and her expedition was predominantly female. The only member of her company to survive the flood, however, was her husband Fintan who turned himself into a salmon. Thus he witnessed all the succeeding invasions of Ireland and was given in many later stories as 'the supreme

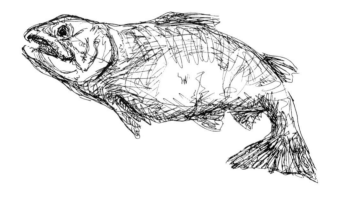

authority in matters of tradition'. A similar story was told of Tuan, son of Starn, who arrived with the second wave of invaders. He lived first as the king of stags, then as an eagle and finally a salmon. It was in this form that he was eaten by the wife of Mac Caireall and reborn as Tuan Mac Caireall. He, like Fintan, witnessed all the great events of history and, relaying them to the writers

and poets of the monastic period, they were duly
preserved for posterity.

When the Milesians (the final group of invaders)
were landing in Ireland, their poet Amairgen
recited a poem in which he identified himself
with the whole of creation. He was a wind, a sea,
a bull, a hawk, a dewdrop, a flower, a boar and a
salmon by turns, 'I am the fairest of flowers. I am
a boar for boldness. I am the salmon in the pool.'
It was said of him that he represented the unity
of all things and that his poems had the power
of creation. With one poem he conjured the fish
into the creeks so that they were rich in fishes ever
after, a theme that again illustrates the creative
power of poetry:

> I invoke the land of Ireland,
> coursed be her fruitful seas,
> fruitful her highlands and her showery woods.

A story told of St Brigid tells of how a beautiful
silver brooch was given into her care by an
unworthy man, who then secretly stole it from her
and tossed it into the sea. He returned looking
for his brooch and not finding it he demanded
that Brigid become his slave. As they were talking,

however, a man came with a fish for Brigid and when the fish was opened the brooch was found inside it. This was a favourite motif in Irish tradition and the story clearly has echoes of the handsome warrior Fraoch, whose story is told in the Ruraiocht, the Ulster cycle of tales.

Fraoch was the son of Be Find, the sister of the goddess Boand, the presiding deity of the River Boyne. He fell in love with Findabar, who gave him the thumb ring which had been given to her by her father. While Fraoch was swimming one day, the cunning Ailill, found the thumb ring in Fraoch's wallet and tossed it in the water. A salmon leapt from the water and caught the ring in its mouth. Ailill, who disapproved of his daughter's relationship with Fraoch, then demanded the restoration of the thumb ring. Fraoch, however, had caught the salmon in secret, so that Findabar's maid brought a platter into the royal house and the salmon was on it. Findabar had cooked it well and the thumb ring lay upon it. After that Ailill, who had been demanding an excessive bride price or dowry for his daughter, consented to the marriage at last, 'I will not set my mind on any other young warrior of Eriu but this one' said Findabar. 'Promise yourself to him then', said Ailill and Medbh.

The god of the sea was Manannán Mac Lir. It was said of him, 'For the space of nine waves he would be submerged in the sea but he would rise again on the crest of the tenth.' In one of his poems he celebrated 'the speckled salmon that leap from the sea, the bright sea on which you look. These are my calves, my brightly coloured lambs. At peace without mutual hostility.'

One colourful tradition says that the mother of St Finan Cam was impregnated by a beautiful golden salmon while swimming in Loch Lein, the lower lake of Killarney, and that this was how the saint was conceived.

Flowers in Irish Myth

In the celebrated tale of the *Destruction of Da Derga's Hostel*, there is a description of a beautiful woman:

> She had a bright silver comb with gold decoration on it and she was washing from a silver vessel with four gold birds on it and shimmering gems of crimson on its rim. She wore a crimson cloak, fastened with a silver brooch coiled with gold; her long hooded tunic was of fine green silk with animal brooches of gold and silver at her breast and shoulders. Men might say that her hair was like the blooming iris in summer or like red gold that has been burnished.

The wild iris, also called the flag, was known by its Irish name Feileastram in many country places. So much so that is was said there was 'no summer without the Feileastram'.

Dian Cécht was the old Irish god of herbs and healing, but he soon grew jealous of his son Miach's abilities. He struck Miach three times with a sword, Miach curing himself each time, but a fourth blow proved fatal. Herbs grew from Miach's grave. There were 365 of them in all, one for each of his joints and sinews. They had magical curative properties, for not only could they cure every illness, but they held the promise of eternal life. Miacóh's sister Airmid, realising their value, laid them out on her cloak in order of their usefulness and importance. The jealous Dian Cécht, however, came and shook the cloak so that the herbs and their secrets would remain a mystery forever.

In another story, Airmid helped her father to guard a well of healing. It was into this well that Dian Cécht put every kind of herb that grew in Ireland. It was known as Topria Slaine and was one of the most famous wells of all. During the second battle of Mag Tuiread, he sang incantations over the well into which he cast the mortally wounded and from which they rose up, restored to life, good as new. Dian Cécht was also credited with fitting the god Midir with a new eye when one of his eyes was put out by a sprig of holly that was hurled at him.

If meat or any other kind of food was inedible in the old days it was said to be 'as tough as taithfheileann'. This was the Irish name for woodbine or honeysuckle, the toughness of its stems almost legendary. No wonder then that when the two champions, Ferdia and Cuchulainn confronted each other at the ford, Cuchulainn was goaded into action when his charioteer said:

Ferdia throws you as the foam is thrown by the river; he grinds you down as the mill would grind the malt, he cuts you down as the axe cuts down the oak, he binds you as the woodbine binds the trees; he pounces on you as the hawk the little birds.

The scent of woodbine in some quiet leafy lane is still very much the essence of summer. It is interesting to note that during their fight, which lasted for three days, Ferdia and Cuchulainn shared their herbs of healing and their food at evening time, 'And for every herb and plant that was put to Cuchulainn's wounds, he sent an equal share westwards over the ford to Ferdia. And of every kind of food that was brought to Ferdia he sent an equal share to Cuchulainn.' It was very strictly forbidden to burn woodbine in a fire. If this were done it betokened bad fortune.

The creamy white flowers of the meadowsweet have long been known for the heaviness of their scent, hence the lovely old saying, 'Meadowsweet in the jar and Maggie asleep on the chair.' One of its names in Irish is 'Crios Cuchulainn', though there does not appear to be any legend to explain why this should be so. Yarrow was said to have been used by the druids in the making of prophecies, especially in regard to weather predictions. The foxglove was known in many parts as fairy fingers or fairy thimbles, illustrating its association with the people of the 'sidhe', the fairy race. The colour of the foxglove was used to express the beauty of the Celtic Otherworld, 'A delight to the eye the number of our hosts, the colour of the foxgloves every cheek.' In the same text we read of those who lived in the Otherworld, 'Their hair is like the blooming primrose, their smooth skin the colour of snow.' When Nera returned from the Otherworld, the primrose is one of the plants he brought with him, the others being wild garlic and golden fern.

In one of the stories told by Caolite to St Patrick, he describes the virtues of a hill called Fionntulach. It was from this hill that the men of the Fianna set out to do battle with the enemies of Ireland at the great mythological battle of Ventry. Caolite recalled with delight 'its beautiful blackberries, haws of the hawthorn, nuts of the hazels of Cantyre'. There too were tender twigs of the bramble as well as sprays of the gentian, all of this with watercress at the beginning of the summer. There are different varieties of gentian, including the field and the marsh gentian, but the spring gentian with its fabulous blue flowers is still very much a feature of the limestone landscape of the Burren, the flowers appearing in early May and June. There were birds in the trackless oak woods, Caolite said, squirrels too, salmon and eels in the rivers and otters in the secret hidden places. The picture he paints of the hill is very simple but lyrical. Elsewhere he says, 'I have seen the gentian bearing meadow with the red deer in their sportiveness.'

The colour of the eyes was often compared to flowers in Irish myth, the bluebell being a firm favourite in such cases. The 'ringing' of the wild bluebells in the woods was sometimes allied to the 'geantrai sidhe', the beautiful fairy music heard at the first of summer. The Great Mullein (or Aaron's Rod) is one of the truly magnificent flowers of high summer. No wonder then that its lovely yellow flowers were sometimes carried as protection against witchcraft and enchantment. The wonderfully soft leaves had more practical uses, for when they were boiled in milk and strained they were used as a cure for consumption. The dried tops of plants were even used to make tapers for fire burning.

Birds in Irish Myth

The robin is the quintessential bird of Christmas and there are few families who do not receive at least one Christmas card with a robin on it. The Irish name for the robin is 'an Spideog' and in Irish tradition it was known as 'Spideog Mhuintir Shuileabhain', illustrating the bird's close association with the O'Sullivan family. The robin was in fact characterised as the champion and supporter of their heroes in battle. It was said that one of their ancestors, Maolughra, gave away an eye as an act of generosity, thus mirroring the generosity of the robin when it plucked the thorns at the Crucifixion.

The robin's practice of building its nest in

peculiar places, such as old kettles and the like, inevitably endeared it to human kind, especially children. Its nest was sacrosanct above all others and those who interfered with it did so at their peril. The wren was far less popular. According to tradition, it betrayed the hero Fionn Mac Cumhail. The latter was hiding in a clump of bushes but as his pursuers drew near, his wren pinched him in the ear with its beak and thus betrayed him. It was said that the little nip was visible in the hero's ear until the time of his death. The wren, which is in fact one of the most widely distributed resident birds of all, is known in Irish as 'an Dreoilín'. Some monastic texts fancifully interpreted the name as meaning 'Draoi Ean', the bird of the druids, adding for good measure lists of predictions said to have been made by the druids based on observations of the wren. The practice of hunting the wren on St Stephen's Day may have stemmed from this clerical antipathy to the bird and its associations with the druids, imagined or otherwise.

The stonechat, known in Irish as 'an Caislin Cloch', had a dispute with the wren, but she could not distinguish him from his fellows. The stonechat, however, tricked him into boasting of his skills as a thresher and so identified him at last. It was the stonechat, the blackbird and the grey cow who defiantly bid goodbye to the cold of March, but the latter borrowed days from April to punish them with cold again. 'Three days for skinning the blackbird, three days for the stonechat too and three for the old grey cow.'

There was a mythical poet and satirist called Aithirne who was known for his miserly ways. He was so selfish that he would never share his food with anyone and would never welcome visitors. In a strange and colourful tale, he visited the Otherworld asking for 'the three herons of refusal and inhospitality' for his own house. One of these told the visitor not to enter, the second told him to leave and the third told him not to come back again. The heron is known in Irish as 'an Corr Riasc' and it was said in many parts that the weather followed the heron. Herons flying south meant the coming of the cold; if they flew north, however, then warmer weather was on the way. The heron is in fact the most patient of fishers and its silhouette in flight – head tucked back, long legs trailing behind – is very distinctive. A relative of the heron, the little egret, has been turning up on Irish shores in recent years.

The jester Comhdan lived in Munster in the seventh century. Sometimes he slept underwater with the fishes, but when he slept on dry land, the birds of the air gathered round him and gave him shelter. There were robins and wrens, blackbirds and thrushes, goldfinches too, the last of these being the birds of healing in old Irish legend. The Munster King Eoghan Mor had a dream in which seven lean and hungry black cows devoured seven handsome white cows. When the druids predicted seven years of plenty followed by seven years of famine, Eoghan had the granaries filled with grain. The famine duly came, and Eoghan distributed the grain as wisely as he could, but reserved some for the birds. One of his prize possessions was a cloak made from the skin of a magic salmon.

The Cailleach Barra was a representation of an earth goddess and protectress of animals and birds. The god of love in Irish myth was Aonghus. The most handsome of all the gods, he changed four of his kisses into four beautiful birds, which had the power to charm the young people of Ireland. Aonghus had a vision of a beautiful young woman in a dream, eventually finding her in the shape of a swan on the waters of Loch Bel Dracon. Aonghus also took the form of a swan, and having embraced, they circled the lake three times before heading off to Brú na Bóinne, where their singing was so beautiful that it lulled the company to sleep for three days and three nights.

In another tale, the god Midir carried off the High King's daughter Etain from the royal fortress at Tara. They too took the form of swans and flew off together to Midir's home at Bri Leith. The story of the transformation of the children of Lir – Aodh, Conn and Fiachra and their sister Fionnuala – into four white swans remains one of the best-loved tales in Irish mythology.

Fintan MacBochra, who came to Ireland with the expedition led by the woman Cessair, underwent transformations too. At one stage he turned himself into an eagle, flying high above the mountains and glens and the lakelets shining below. Fintan had great knowledge of Ireland, 'I know of her feasts and her cattle raids; I know of her discords and wars, her loves and romances too.'

The curlew, like the blackbird, was known to whistle for rain, and the early arrival of wild geese was taken as a token of a prolonged and severe winter. The Fianna were depicted very much as nature lovers and were identified with birds such as the blackbird and the cuckoo. In 'Fionn's song in praise of May', there is a verse:

Now comes the bird of dusky hue,
The loud cuckoo, the summer lover;
The branching trees and thick with leaves,
The bitter, evil time is over.

Conaire Mor was a mythical King of Tara. On the death of the old king, a great flock of birds flew over Conaire's chariot. The birds were marvellously coloured but when Conaire took a sling to make a cast at them they were changed into human form. One of their number told him that he was never to make a cast at birds and urged him to go to Tara where he would be installed as High King. Conaire's motto was, 'I will enquire of wise men that I may myself be wise.' The goddess Morrigan was also known as the Badb, the scaldcrow of battle. It was said that her fruit crop was the heads of the slain.

Irish saints were also associated with the wild birds of the countryside. The swans on the Lakes of Killarney came to the call of St Cainneach, while those on Lough Foyle did the same for Comhghall. It was the blackbird, however, who made its nest on one of the outstretched palms of St Kevin of Glendalough when the latter was fasting and praying for Lent. So fond was the saint of the blackbird that he did not move till her young were reared. According to one version, 'he made himself a tree for the little bird'. This tradition inspired the poet Seamus Heaney to write a poem about it.

Animals in Irish Myth

Two of the most celebrated horses in Irish mythology were the Grey of Macha and the Black of Saingliu, both born at the time of the birth of Cuchulainn. The newly born foals were in fact presented as gifts to the baby boy. In the story of the hero's death, the majestic Grey resisted all attempts to be harnessed. Cuchulainn's charioteer interpreted this as an omen of bad fortune. When Cuchulainn began to reproach the horse, the latter came to him and shed tears of blood. When the battle got underway, Erc, King of Leinster, launched a spear at Cuchulainn but it struck the Grey instead, and though Cuchulainn withdrew

the spear, the wounded Grey galloped away with part of the shattered harness still dangling about him.

The celebrated Brown Bull of Ulster was coveted by Queen Medbh of Connaught and so began the enmity between the two provinces. At the end of the saga, the White Bull of Connaught and the Brown Bull of Ulster faced each other in deadly combat, the Brown Bull gaining the upper hand in the end.

In an earlier story, when the Dagda, the father of all the gods, asked Bres of the Fomoir for a heifer, Bres thought it a very foolish request. In a little while, however, the heifer began to low to her calf and it was that lowing that summoned back all the cattle of Ireland that had been demanded in tribute during the reign of the tempestuous Bres.

Mongan was one of the most colourful characters in Irish myth. He was the son of Manannán Mac Lir, the god of the sea who made love to the wife of Fiachna, King of Ulster. One of his greatest claims to fame was his ability to change shape, a favourite motif in Irish legend, 'He will be in the shape of every beast on the azure sea and on the land. He will be a dragon before the hosts; he will be a wolf of every great forest.' This was no great wonder, for the little boy was barely three days old when his father, Manannán, came and took him to be reared in the Otherworld until he was twelve years of age. In later times, it was the warrior of the Fianna Caoilte who came to confirm a story told by Mongan when this was contradicted by one of the poets.

Caoilte himself was at the very centre of another animal story, the story of the straggling drove. Finn attempted to seize power at Tara and was duly arrested by the High King Cormac. Caoilte wreaked havoc on the environs of Tara

and then, disguising himself as a servant, he held
the candle at a banquet in the great hall. Despite
the disguise, Cormac recognised him, saying, 'It is
Caoilte's eyes I see [reflected in] my candlestick.'
'Tell me how I can gain freedom for my master',
said Caoilte. It was then that Cormac demanded
the great straggling drove which was to consist of
a couple of all the wild creatures of Ireland. There
are clear echoes here of the biblical tale of Noah's
Ark. Cormac, in making his demands, however,
was confident that no one, not even Caoilte
could create such a drove.

According to the story, Caoilte travelled the
length and breadth of Ireland in search of the
wild creatures for his drove, amongst them two

foxes from Sliabh Cuilinn, two wild oxen from the Burren, two rabbits from Sidhe Dubh Donn, two bats from Pluais na Cno, two badgers from Ulster, two pigs from the pigs of the sons of Lir, a ram and a crimson sheep. Caoilte had great difficulty keeping all the animals and birds together but eventually managed to bring them to Tara. The king, however, had another ruse in store for him. He was far too busy then to inspect the drove, so Caolite would have to keep watch on his company till morning time. To add to Caoilte's woes, Cormac insisted that the animals be lodged in a house with nine doors. In these circumstances, it was no great wonder that many of the animals made yet more attempts to escape and were it not for the athleticism of Caoilte himself running round and round the house all night long, they would surely have done so. When morning came, Cormac duly inspected the animals, 'But all the good it did him was to see them together for that one time, for no sooner did Finn get his freedom than the whole company of them scattered here and there and no two of them went by the same road out of Tara.' This marvellously colourful tale became the inspiration for many later folktales, among them the story of the man who brings a husk of hares to Tara and again lodges them in the house with nine doors. Hares with one ear were really witches under enchantment; white rabbits were the spirits of the dead returned to life in that form.

One day, when the Fianna were coming home from hunting, Finn and his two favourite hounds, Bran and Sceolan, came upon a beautiful deer, which curiously the hounds did not chase. Instead, they played with it affectionately, licking its neck and its face. That evening, a beautiful woman came to Finn, revealing that she herself was the wild deer, forced to live like that because she had refused the love of Fear Dorcha, the dark druid. Her name was Sadbh. Finn fell in love with her and they were happy. But when Finn was away one day, the druid came back with a magic hazel rod and turned her back into a deer. Finn searched high and low for her but all to no avail. After seven years Finn and his men were hunting on Ben Gulban when they came upon a little boy who told them that he had been reared by a deer. Finn recognised him as his own son and gave him the name Oisin, a name which means 'little deer'. Oisin's son in turn was called Oscar, 'deer lover'.

Another mythical character, Tadhg Mac Cian

was forbidden to eat the meat of badgers but his son Cormac had a badger killed and served at a feast in his father's honour. Tadhg was less than impressed, however, and had his son banished from court. The modern Irish word for badger is 'broc' but the earlier word 'Tadc' makes it the antecedent for the human 'Tadhg'. The same Tadhg later visited the Otherworld and among the islands he visited was one with huge sheep.

Trees in Irish Myth

The rowan was the tree *par excellence* of Irish myth and legend. It was on wattles of rowan that the druids slept in order to have prophetic visions of the future. The brilliance of the red berries in autumn imbued the tree with magical powers, hence its association with the druids and all things magical. The wattles of the rowan were sometimes carved with Ogham symbols to further enhance their powers. No wonder, then, that the rowan was called 'fid na ndraoi', the tree of the druids. It figures prominently in many Irish myths and legends.

In *The Cattle Raid of Fraoch*, Fraoch, the most

handsome warrior in Ireland, sets off to woo
Findabar, the beautiful daughter of Ailill and
Medbh of Connaught, but Ailill is less than keen
on the match and so demands a bride price of
'three score dark grey horses with golden bridles
and twelve milch cows and a white calf with red
ears'. Fraoch refuses and Ailill plots his downfall,
asking him to swim to the far side of the river,
'Bring me a branch of the rowan that grows on
the river bank. I find its berries beautiful.' There
follows a lyrical description of Fraoch returning
with the rowan branch, 'Findabar said after that,
whatever looked beautiful to her, she thought
it more beautiful to look at Fraoch across the
dark waters, his skin fair, his hair shining, his
eyes very blue, the branch with the red berries
between his throat and his fair face.' Ailill asked
for a second branch of rowan and Fraoch turned
to cross the river again. This time, however, he
was attacked by the river monster but Findabar
threw him a sword with which he cut off the
monster's head.

In *The Pursuit of Diarmuid and Gráinne*, the giant
Searbhan guards a magical rowan in the woods of
Dubhros. The tree grew from one of the berries
dropped by the magical Tuatha De Dannann and

was guarded by Searbhan the giant. Gráinne begs to have some of the berries from the tree and Diarmuid is forced to slay the giant to bring them to her.

In Irish folklore it was held that the first man was created from an alder tree, the first woman from a rowan tree. This was why a sprig of rowan or alder was placed above the cradle, depending on the sex of the child. Sprigs of rowan were also tied to cows' tails or twined round the churn to protect the workings of the dairy on May Eve, a time of heightened activity among the spirits and the fairies.

The hazel tree was also important in myth and legend. Over the Well of Segais grew the nine hazels of wisdom, 'from which came the knowledge of the sages'. The hazelnuts dropped into the well and were eaten by the Salmon of Knowledge, the celebrated bradán feasa of Irish legend. It was the bradán feasa that gave Finn Mac Cumhail his great knowledge and so Finn had reasons of his own to be thankful to the hazel. Another mythological character, Mac Cuill was the husband of the goddess Banba. His name means 'son of the hazel'. In later times a rod of hazel was a protection against evil spirits of all kinds. It was also a popular choice among water diviners when they were trying to locate a well.

In Celtic myth, the birch tree was associated with love, romance and the month of May, 'Come, come to the spreading birch, the spirit of the trees and the cuckoo.' Ailill and Medbh had seven sons all called Maine. When one of them got married, the halls were decorated with branches of birch. Manannán Mac Lir, the god of the sea, lived on a beautiful island, Emhain Abhlach. Here grew marvellous apple trees, all of them hung with golden fruit. In one story, Manannán visits Cormac Mac Airt at Tara, bringing with him a silver branch with golden apples. When the branch is shaken, so beautiful is its music that all who hear it are lulled to sleep. Similarly, a beautiful woman of the Otherworld brings a branch of the fabulous tree to Bran, urging him to set out on his magical voyage.

The elm tree was associated with Irish saints, among them St Ruadhan who had one such tree at his monastery. The tree was famous for dripping a honey-like substance that tasted more and more beautiful. According to the old saying, 'Tis a wedge of the elm that splits itself.' One of the most popular beliefs about the ash tree was that a fire of ash could banish evil. The ash, like the hawthorn, was frequently associated with the holy well. In mythological times, the trees at sacred wells were called the trees of Medbh, illustrating the connection between the ash and Queen Medbh. Ash was very much used in the making of country furniture in later times. The oak was associated

with St Brigid of Cill Dara, the church of the
oak. The tree was also the symbol of kingship. It
was said of the good King Conaire Mor, 'There
was great bounty in his reign: acorns up to the
knees every autumn, a surfeit over the Buas and
the Boand.'

King Labhraid Loinseach had horse's ears, a
widow's son discovering his secret when he went
to cut his hair. On the advice of a druid, the
young barber told the secret to a tree, a weeping
willow by a pool, but when the tree was cut down
and made into a harp, the latter revealed the
king's secret every time it was played.

The hawthorn was the fairy tree and the poets
stood with their backs to it when reciting a satire
against the local chieftain. When the Maines,
the sons of Ailill and Medbh, were in trouble,
however, it was with a fence of bramble and
blackthorn they protected themselves. Wands
of yew were used in rituals. One of the most
popular yew trees was at Muckross Abbey,
Killarney. The stories about it were more than
popular with Victorian guides and tourists alike.
Holly was the tree of protection, an emblem of
abundance too, its bright red berries feeding the
birds of the air. The mistletoe was neither shrub

nor tree and did not grow on the ground. In this way it defied convention and those who stood under its boughs were free of convention too. All this was just a part of the magic of trees in Irish myth and legend.

Apples in Irish Myth

The story of the *Destruction of Da Derga's Hostel* is essentially the story of the death of a king. It is long and dramatic and full of the portents of impending doom. In one scene, the king's fool, the court jester is described:

> Gold ear rings in his ears, a cloak of many colours he had on. Nine swords in his hands and nine silver shields and nine apples of gold. He threw up the swords and shields and apples, and only one remained in his hands but none touched the ground and their progress was like that of bees going by on a beautiful day. When I saw him, he was at

his most brilliant, but then all of a sudden everything fell to the floor and a great clatter rose around him.

After a brief pause, the fool took the swords, the shields and the apples and began to juggle with them again but the same thing happened again. They fell to the floor once more and this was taken as a token of things to come. In the same story, another of the strange and intriguing characters who entered the hostel during the king's stay is described as having 'hair rough and bristly, so that if a sack full of wild apples was emptied over it, each apple would stick to the hair and none would fall to the ground'.

The apple was very much a symbol of abundance and plenty in Irish myth and legend. The god of the sea, Manannán Mac Lir, lived on a fabulous island called 'Emhain Abhlach', Emhain of the trees. These were no ordinary trees – they were trees of magic and enchantment and healing too, 'A wood without fault, without withering, the leaves the colour of gold.' One of the human visitors to this beautiful apple kingdom was Tadhg Mac Cian who described the sweet smell of crimson branches in the wood, 'They went on through the wood till they came to an apple garden full of red apples and leafy oaks and hazels yellow with nuts.' It was a wonder to him, he said, that it was summer among the apple trees at Emhain when it was winter at home. There were trees too with great purple berries shining with splendour and ripeness. In one of the scenes, the company come upon two young lovers on a hilltop. The young man had a sweet smelling apple in his hand and the apple was the colour of gold and though he ate a third part of it, every time it never became less. The youth turned out to be Connla, who had also been tempted to visit the paradise of apples. Soon afterwards, Tadhg and his company come upon a house with a great sheltering tree nearby, which is both clothed in blossom and hung with fruit: a favourite motif for magic and enchantment in Irish myth. When Tadhg wonders about the marvellous tree, it is Connla's companion who tells him that the fruit of the tree sustains the entire household, 'And it was an apple of that apple tree that brought Connla here to me: A good tree it is with its white blossomed branches and golden apples.' Connla had in fact survived for a whole month on one of the magic apples of the tree before setting out on his journey to the island paradise. There were beautiful birds on the island too, and they, like their human neighbours, thrived on the apples, 'The music that they made would put men sick at heart at their ease.' An admirer of Cuchulainn said of him once:

> Fifty gold apples playing overhead,
> playing tricks on his breath;
> As a king his like is not to be found,
> not among the gentle, not among the fierce.

It was the virtue of the king above all which determined the abundance or otherwise of the fruit. Of one it was said, 'It is in his reign that we have the three crowns of Eriu, the crown of corn, the crown of flowers and the crown of acorns. Since he became king, no cloud has obscured the sun from the middle of spring to the middle of autumn.' In the story of the wedding of Maine

Mongor, a son of King Ailill and Queen Medbh of Connaught, his company is described as being:

> ... handsome and stately, their cheeks like the flowers of the woods in May or like the foxgloves on the mountain. There were seven greyhounds following his chariot and on every chain of theirs was a golden apple. And the people of the house laid down green-leaved birch and rushes before them.

When Cael, the handsome warrior of the Fianna recited a poem in honour of his beloved, the beautiful Cred, he too made reference to the apple, 'There is a vat of royal bronze where flows the pleasant juice of malt. An apple tree stands over it, its branches laden down with fruit. When Cred's cup is filled from the vat, four apples fall into it at one time together.'

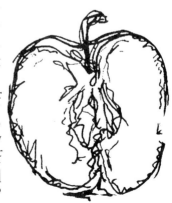

When the children of Tuirenn, Brian, Iuchar, Iucharbe, unwittingly killed Cian, the father of Lugh, Lugh demanded the payment of an 'eric'

or fine – literally compensation. One of his demands was that they bring him back three apples from the gardens of the East:

> ...there are no apples in the world like them, for each is the colour of burnished gold and each is the size of the head of a child a month old and they have the taste of honey on them. If anyone who has sickness eats of them, he is made well again and though they are eaten forever they are never made less.

Brave though the three sons were, Lugh doubted very much if they could take the apples from those who guarded them, for it had been prophesied that three young warriors from the west would come to take the apples and so the guard had been redoubled. They sailed in a small boat, a currach, to the gardens of the East and though his brothers favoured a direct attack, Brian suggested they turn into hawks and snatch the apples that way. This was exactly what they did and though the three daughters of the king, famed sorceresses, gave chase after them, they escaped by means of another transformation, this time into swans.

Suibhne Geilt, driven mad by the horrors of

battles, survived on wild apples, blackberries and cress though he was not very fond of the briars. They did not give him fair terms, he said. They were forever tearing his skin and they had the fill of his blood. It was W.B. Yeats who wrote of 'The silver apples of the moon, the golden apples of the sun', in his poem 'The Dream of Wandering Aengus', which was clearly inspired by Irish myth and legend. When Senchan and the poets visited the generous King Guaire, they made impossible demands, one a demand for blackberries in winter.

Snow in Irish Myth

While Cuchulainn and Loeg his charioteer were speaking, a marvellous heavy snow fell on the Ulaid, and it was as high as the shoulders of the men and the shafts of their chariots. Great work was done by the charioteers of the Ulaid then in putting up stone columns to shelter their horses from the snow. These shelters were called 'the stables of the horses of the Ulaid', and they are still there to this day, as proof of the story. This is a scene from the old Irish myth *The Intoxication of the Ulaid*, one of the most colourful tales of them all. Conchobar, King of Ulster was invited to two different feasts on the one night, one prepared by Findtan, the other by Cuchulainn. The king did not wish to offend either; his solution, to spend the first part of the night with Findtan, the second with Cuchulainn. At midnight, they duly left for Cuchulainn's feast but they soon went astray and found themselves heading south and west. 'Never before have we taken this route from Dun Da Bend to Dun Delgan', said the king, and he was right. They had in fact strayed far beyond the borders of Ulster and were in the territory of Cu Roi, King of Munster, when the snow began to fall and so after some discussion they headed for his fortress at Temuir Luachra. Two Druids, Cromm Darail and Cromm Deroil, standing on the ramparts, were amazed at the sight of the approaching army and argued over what they were actually seeing. Cromm Darail thought it was no more than the great oaks and the royal strongholds, the deer and wild beasts with their horns and antlers overhead. He even suggested that it might be no more than the flurries of snow. 'They seem to me not flurries of snow', said his companion, 'but distant men arriving in companies with their great spears and crimson shields.' The Druids, whose part in the story is very much one of light relief, soon fell in a faint at the sight of the approaching hordes. Cromm Darail fell over the wall and landed on the outside, while his companion Cromm Deroil fell off the wall, landing on the inside. Nonetheless, it was the latter who first saw the great host at close quarters, 'They descended from their horses and sat upon the green as one man, the heat of their bodies so great that the snow softened and melted for a great distance on every side.' A battle ensued between the inhabitants of the fortress and the Ulaid. It was the Ulaid who eventually gained the upperhand, and heading home, Cuchulainn entertained them with a magnificent feast that lasted for all of forty days and forty nights.

In the story of the *Exile of the Sons of Uisneach*, the beautiful Deirdre was put into fosterage until the time would come when she would marry the King Conchobar. One day in winter, however, Deirdre sees her foster father killing a calf in the snow and a raven drinking the blood, whereupon she said to her attendant Leabharcam, 'My love is for a man with those three colours: Hair like the raven, cheeks like the blood, skin like the snow.' 'Then luck and good fortune are yours', said Leabharcam in reply, 'for such a man is not far off. He is Naoise, son of Uisneach.' 'I will not

be happy till I see him', said Deirdre. She was
promised to the king but eloped with Naoise to
Scotland, his brothers Ainle and Ardan fleeing
too. After some time, Conchobar, the King,
feigning forgiveness invited them home again but
had the brothers killed in an act of treachery.
Deirdre subsequently took her own life.

The story of *The Children of Lir* is one of the
best-loved of all the old Irish myths and legends.
Their stepmother, Aoife, turns the children,
Aodh, Conn, Fiachra and Fionnuala into four
beautiful swans, forcing them to spend 300 years
on Loch Dairbhreach, another 300 on Sruth na
Maoile, and a final 300 at Iorrus Domnann. It

was on Sruth na Maoile (the Sea of Moyle) that the swans endured the greatest hardship of all:

> There came a night on them, the like of which they had never known before for frost and snow and wind and cold. And they were crying at the hardness of the wind and the greatness of the snow. When they came to Carraig na Ron, the water froze around them, and their feathers stuck to the rock the way they were not able to move from it at all.

Many of the stories of the Fianna were stories of hunting and enchantments. One day the Fianna were hunting on the island of Toraig to the north when they raised a beautiful fawn. They gave chase after it and followed it through the whole country till they came to Slaibh na mBan, where the fawn put down its head and disappeared underground. It was then that a heavy snow began to fall which bent down the tops of the trees and the courage and strength went from the Fianna with the dint of the bad weather and Finn said to Caoilte, 'Is there any place we can find shelter tonight?' Caoilte went to the brow of the hill and seeing a beautiful house full of lights, he made for it at once, though he knew it was a house of the sidhe (a house of the fairy race). When he went inside he found a beautiful company, some of whom made ready to entertain him, but he went back for Finn and the rest of the Fianna. 'It is a long time you were away from us', said Finn, 'for never since I took up arms have I known a night as snowy as this.' The Fianna were royally entertained by their hosts who turned out to be Don Mac Midir and his brothers. Then Finn and his men sided with their hosts against their enemies and defeated them in battle after which Don revealed that he had sent out a beautiful young woman in the shape of a fawn to tempt the Fianna to his bruigh (fairy palace).

There are many stories of St Patrick in contention with the druids. One of his main rivals was Lucet Maol who waved his magic wand of rowan and covered the plain with snow as far as the eye could see. It was the loveliest sight, the brilliance of the snow glistening and gleaming far and away. When St Patrick asked the druid to remove the snow again, however, he could not do so, so Patrick himself had to do it with a blessing and a prayer. When haws and berries were plentiful, the druids predicted heavy snows, for the haws were seen as provision for the birds in the hardship to come.

Wells in Irish Myth

Wells and water, the sustainer of life, were very much part of the magic of Irish myth and legend. In *Agallamh na Seanorach*, Caoilte, one of the leaders of the Fianna, describes the beauty of the well of Tradaban to St Patrick. It was a magical place filled with cress of the purest kind, but being neglected somewhat, its beautiful brooklime had not grown. Brooklime is in fact a handsome plant with spikes of deep blue flowers that complement its glossy green foliage. It is one of the Speedwells and favours the same habitats as watercress, the latter well known as a salad plant or garnish. There were trout on the banks of the well, wild swine in the wilderness around it, and

wild deer in the woods with their magical fawns. There was mast on the trees and fishes in the streams and the finest sprays of arum lily everywhere around. It was only fitting, then, that Caoilte should celebrate the beauty of the place in verse. Elsewhere, Caoilte mentions the eating of cress by the Fianna.

It was to the Well of Uisneach, however that Oisin went in search of water for a feast. Uisneach, which had associations with the druids, was said to mark the centre of Ireland, the country then divided into five, not four, ancient provinces. The lighting of fires was very much part of the ritual there but it was its famous well that attracted Oisin. According to the story, he went to the well 'with his face behind him so that no one should find the way'. There were eight salmon in the well when he found it at last, eight salmon gloriously stippled with silvers and shades of every kind, the well so remote from human activity that they had nothing to fear at all. He took some of the watercress and brooklime, and dipping a pail into it, he claimed some of the salmon as his own. When he went back, he prepared a feast for the King of Ireland, so that the night was spent not just in feasting but in storytelling too. The Well of Uisneach has echoes of the Well of Knowledge, over which the nine hazels of wisdom grew.

In the Second Battle of Mag Tuired, the god of healing, Dian Cécht sings incantations over a well so that even those who were mortally wounded were restored to life by morning. This clearly identifies him with the cult of healing springs, though he was also very much associated with the magic of herbs and the like. One text describes him as the sage of leechcraft. It was his daughter Airmid who helped him guard the magic well. The Second Battle of Mag Tuired was fought between the Tuatha De Danann and their enemies, the Fomoir. The latter, knowing nothing of the sacred well, were astounded to see those whom they killed one day in the thick of battle the next. The text has Dian Cécht and his daughter not only chanting spells over the well but tossing into it the most secret, the most magnificent of herbs, so that not only were the dead restored to life, they returned to battle with a renewed ardour.

Another version tells how Ruadhan, one of the Fomoir, succeeded in obtaining from Goibniu, the smith-god, a magic spear which the craft god, Credne, duly fitted with rivets. As soon as he had the spear in his hands however, he turned and threw it at Goibniu, wounding him badly. Goibniu pulled out the spear and making a cast at Ruadhan, killed him in an instant. As for Goibniu himself, he went into the well and was healed overnight. Some versions have for good measure one of the sons of Indech, a Fomorian king, coming to the well with his followers, each of them bearing a stone, which they threw into the well until the water dried up and a great cairn was raised over it, 'And they came with stones and threw them into the well till there was nothing of the water, the fabled water of healing and renown.'

In Finn's poem in praise of the month of May, he talks of the waterfall, high and lonely, awaiting the embrace of the warm-hearted pool below. It was the time when the music of the woods was playing and colour was painted on every hill. Oisin, remembering Finn, spoke of his love of nature; he loved the blackbird of Doire Chairn more than he would ever have loved the ringing of the bells. Cael, in his poem of praise for his beloved Cred, describes the well before her house, framed as it was by a railing of crystal and carbuncle gems.

Wells were very much part of the magic of the Otherworld too. One account describes a fabled well with marvellously coloured cloths around, and on each cloth a pin of purest gold. The saints, too, were associated with wells. During the time of St Flannan there were plenty of fish in the rivers, plenty of fruits on the trees and plenty of water in the wells. Flannan was an abbot at Killaloe, the legends clearly implying that his goodness was reflected in the bounty of nature.

Many holy wells had a sacred trout in them; those who were lucky enough to see it were assured of good fortune in life. Wells sometimes sprang from the ground when a child, destined to become a saint, was about to be baptised. The water from the well was then used in the baptism ceremony. The veneration of holy wells has echoes of the druids and their regard for them. There were two wells which were the wells of riches and poverty. The trouble was, there was no way of telling them apart.

The Four Seasons:
The Celtic Year

There were four major festivals in the Celtic year: Imbolc, which marked the beginning of spring; Beltaine, which welcomed summer; Lughnasa, giving thanks for the harvest, and Samhain, which coincided with the beginning of winter and was essentially the eve of the New Year. The festival of Imbolc was dedicated to the goddess Brigit. Brigit was characterised as the goddess of healing and of smiths, and also as the goddess of fertility and poetry. She was linked with the gods of artistic skill: Goibhniu, the smith; Lughta the wright, and Credne Cred, the metal worker.

She was associated with light and the movement of the sun. The word Imbolc is sometimes given as 'sheep's milk', reflecting the association with the fertility of spring. In *Cormac's Glosssary* Brigit is described as 'a poetess, a goddess whom the poets worshipped'. There were other goddesses of fertility such as the goddess Danu, whose name is preserved in the Kerry mountains known as the Paps, Da Chich Anann. In *Cormac's Glossary* she is listed as the mother of the gods, 'mater deorum Hibernensium', while another text has her as the goddess of prosperity to whom the province of Munster owed its fertility. Her identification with the earth is clearly seen in the name of her mountains.

Imbolc effectively divided the winter half of the year into winter and spring. Then came Beltaine, 1 May, the festival of summer, which was generally marked with the lighting of bonfires. It was a time when praise was offered to Bel, the light giver, and the druids rekindled the fires from ceremonial torches. According to one ancient text, 'A fire was kindled in his name at the beginning of summer and the cattle driven through it.' The rays of sun were sometimes thought of as 'the sacred fires of Bel', again stressing the association with brightness and light. *Cormac's Glossary* says that the Beltaine fires served to preserve cattle from diseases, adding that the druids chanted their magic spells over them. The lighting of fires at Beltaine continued in some districts well into modern times. The name Beltaine is translated by some as 'shining fire'.

If Imbolc divided the winter half of the year into winter and spring, then Lughnasa (1 August) divided the summer half into summer and autumn. Lughnasa was the feast of the god Lugh and celebrated the coming of the harvest. It was Lugh himself who instituted the festival to commemorate the foster mother, Tailtiu, 'After Tailtiu died, her name was given to the place and the festival made every year by her foster son Lugh.' The latter was in fact one of the most celebrated of all the gods and skilled in many arts. When he came to Tara for the first time he was introduced as Lugh Samildánach, the man of each and every art. He was sometimes called 'the Shining One', the sun god of genius and light. Through the holding of the festival the people were assured of 'an abundance of corn and milk, freedom from conquest, righteous laws, comfort in every home, fruit in plenty and fishes in the lakes and rivers and streams'. Neglect of the festival, however, meant lean times ahead, 'Kings without keenness or merriment, without hospitality or truth.' In later times, the festival of Lughnasa took on a variety of different names. These included Garland Sunday, Colcannon Sunday, Rock Sunday and Lough Sunday, most if not all being celebrated on the last Sunday in July. The festival was often celebrated on hilltops, or on other elevated sites, though riversides and lakesides were also popular. There are accounts of people leading their horses into lakes, for instance, 'and causing them to swim there as a kind of protection for the coming year'.

Samhain, which literally means the end of the summer, heralded the beginning of the Celtic New Year. It was the time when the boundaries of the sidhe (the spirit world) were thrown open and communion with the spirits was at its most intense. There was emphasis on divination too, that is to say prophecy and the foretelling of the future. Some of the most significant events in Irish myth and legend took place at Samhain. It was the time, for instance, when the Tuatha De Dannann defeated their arch rivals, the Fomoir in the great mythological battle of Mag Tuiread. It was the time when the hero Cuchulainn was visited by the two beautiful women of the sidhe, Li Ban and Fand.

The lighting of the fires was an essential part of the festival, those on the hill of Tlachtga being among the most significant. It was said of the gathering at Tara, 'Three days before Samhain at all times, and three days by ancient custom did the hosts of high renown continue to feast for the whole week.' It has been said that Samhain represented the dissolution of the old order as a prelude to its recreation in the new year to come.

Thus the Celtic year was very much influenced

by the seasons, the annual round of country life, as well as in many instances by the movements, or apparent movements of the sun.

The Land of Promise

It was called Tír Tairnigiri, the Land of Promise,
Tír na mBeo , the Land of the Living, and Tír na
nÓg, the Land of Youth. It was the Otherworld
of the ancient Irish, accessible at Samhain,
November's Eve, through enchanted caves and
the like, or at other times by means of marvellous
voyages. When Nera visited the Otherworld
through the enchanted cave of Cruachan, he
had a vision of the royal fortress in flames but
it was only a premonition, a warning. He set
about retuning home but before he did so he
gathered wild garlic, primrose and golden fern to
substantiate his story. These were the things of
the summer and when he brought them back to

the world of men in dark November it was taken as proof, proof positive that he had indeed been with the people of the sidhe, the people of the Otherworld.

Some of the descriptions of the Otherworld in the voyage tales in particular are wonderfully lyrical. These voyages were called 'imrama' and invariably involved visits to numerous Otherworld islands, each of which was stranger and more fascinating still. The titles of at least seven or eight of the voyage tales are mentioned in old Irish literature but only some of them survive. These include *The Voyage of Bran*, *The Voyage of Maeldun*, *The Voyage of UiChorra* and *The Voyage of Snedgus and Mac Riagla*. There are descriptions of the beautiful Otherworld in other texts, however. The god Midir describes it very lyrically in a story called *Tochmarc Etain* (*The Wooing of Etain*):

There, there is neither mine nor thine: bright the teeth there, dark the brows;
A delight to the eye, the number of our hosts: the colour of foxgloves every cheek;
Purple the surface of every plain: a marvel to see the blackbird's eggs;

Though the plain of Fal [Ireland] be beautiful, it is
desolate compared to this.
Fine the mead of Inis Fail, more wonderful still the
mead of Magh Mar;
A beautiful land it is I tell you of: youth does not
give way to old age.

The land of promise therefore was full of the
delights of nature; brightly coloured birds
filling the place with song from the branches of
marvellous trees, the music of streams echoing
too. One day, when Bran Mac Febhal was walking
near his fort, he found a branch of silver clothed
with white blossoms on the ground before him.
He took the branch indoors and in a little while
a beautiful woman came to him inviting him to
the Land of Promise:

There is a distant isle around which the sea horses
glisten,
A bright course where the white wave surges: Four
pedestals uphold it;
Pillars of white bronze beneath it, they shine
through the ages of beauty;
A lovely land through the ages of the world: this is
the place where many blossoms fall.

It is a world, she tells him, where sorrow, sickness and treachery are unknown, 'In the many coloured land of surpassing beauty, they expect neither decay nor death.' She urged him then not to fall on a bed of sloth but to make preparations for his voyage at once. The day after, Bran set sail, taking with him 'three companies of nine', a magic number. A few days later he met with Manannán Mac Lir riding in a two-wheeled chariot over the sea. He too referred to the Otherworld as a plain of delights, a place of many flowers and marvellous fruits. There was even a beautiful wood under Bran's currach, a wood which Bran did not see at all.

While Bran brought back tidings of only two islands, *The Voyage of Maeldun* took in over thirty islands, most, if not all of them, intriguing and strange. One, for instance had an arch of water that looked like a rainbow full of salmon, rising on one side and falling on the other. Another island had huge cattle and giant swine, another, enchanted trees laden down with the most marvellous fruits and berries. The Otherworld, of course, went beyond the limitations of ordinary time; it simply had no meaning there so that what might seem like a short time to the voyagers might in fact be hundreds of years.

The High King Cormac Mac Airt was another granted the privilege of visiting the Otherworld. He came to it not by means of a wonderful voyage but through a magic mist. Again he saw the strangest of sights. One was a house of silver half thatched with the feathers of white birds, but when the thatchers set to work again, their efforts were in vain for the wind came and blew the feathers away.

This was intended to represent, he found out later, the folly of gathering and hoarding material things. He also visited the Well of Knowledge, the five streams that flowed from it representing the five senses, 'And no one shall have knowledge who does not drink of the well and the streams. They shall have many crafts, those who drink of them both.' The well had its counterpart in the human world, being variously given as the source of the Boyne and the Shannon. Over it grew the nine hazels of wisdom and when the hazelnuts dropped down they produced 'bubbles of mystic inspiration'. During his visit to the Otherworld, Cormac was given the golden cup of truth, which fell asunder when lies were told before it but which was made whole again by truth.

Oisin's sojourn in Tír na nÓg is well known but it was Cuchulainn's charioteer who described it so vividly:

> At the door to the west, where the sun sets, a herd of grey horses, bright their manes and a herd of chestnut horses too.
> At the door to the east, three trees of shining crystal, from where the calls of birds come gently to those within.
> A tree to the west, a tree of silver in the setting sun, radiant and shining with light.

The old Irish myths and sagas give us wonderful glimpses, then, of a world out of time, a world of colour and imagining and beauty.

Nature Lovers

Guaire Aidne was a historical (as distinct from a mythical) King of Connaught who came to power in the middle of the seventh century. His greatest claim to fame was his generosity. Despite this, he was often put upon by the poets and especially by their leader, Senchan. It was a time when the poets held great sway and if they felt they were hard done by in any way, they soon satirised their host and so dishonoured his name. When Senchan and his entourage came to stay with Guaire, they found fault with everything, even the servants and their lineage. It was left to Guaire's brother Marbhan to try and cope with the troublesome guests, known collectively in Irish as a 'trodamh' (literally difficult company). He did everything he could to try and satisfy their demands but still they were not happy. Then he contended with them in riddles to test their poetic skills, one of those doing battle with him being the

poet Dael Duiled. Marbhan then asked to hear 'the poetic croon', an effect notoriously difficult to achieve, and finally he asked for the story of Táin Bó Cúailnge, the story of the brown bull of Cúailnge, which saw the forces of Connaught and Ulster pitted against one another in mortal combat. However, most of the poets could only remember fragments of the tale, whereupon Marbhan advised them to go to the grave of the hero Fergus Mac Róich, where the spirit of Fergus would tell them the story in its entirety. This they did and having done so Marbhan ordered them all to return to their own territories and never to return as a tromdhamh again.

Marbhan may in fact have been a fictional or mythical character, an invention of a later date. Despite his connections with the royal household, he chose to live the life of a swineherd and follow the path of solitude. He was known as a great lover of nature and so when his brother Guaire asked him why he preferred to sleep in the woods when he might have a comfortable bed, he celebrated nature in all its richness and diversity. He had a hut in the woods, he said, with an ash tree on one side and a hazel on the other. His hut was small and yet not small at all. A blackbird sang from its gable while the stags ran through the streams before it. He asked Guaire if he would like to come and see it, for his life there had been happy, very happy, even without the support of his brother. He described the beauty of the yew trees, the oaks and the apples, which were like those that grew in fairy dwellings. There were beautiful wells and waterfalls too, and berries of every kind. The animals were his friends; they were all around him, wild goats and deer and badgers and more, 'Together in bands, a great gathering of the woods, a great gathering comes to my house; foxes come to the woods before it; it is a wonderful sight.' The fox is of course one of the most handsome of all the animals of the Irish countryside. According to tradition, they were originally the dogs of the Norsemen.

There were fish in the rivers, Marbhan said, trout and salmon in the purest of water, honey, wild strawberries and 'arches of bramble with fine blackberries'. The picture he painted was vivid and lyrical. He loved it when summer came, for then it was as if the earth put on a cloak, a mantle of the wildest, most wonderful green. Meanwhile the pigeons were happy to coo at his door, the thrushes to sing in the green boughs above. He referred too to the wild geese that came in the winter time – barnacle geese and brent geese. They came shortly before Samhain, one of the greatest feasts in the Celtic year. A linnet sang to him from the boughs of a hazel tree, its song like the song of enchantment, while the white birds, the herons and the gulls crossed overhead, the sea singing to them all the while. He was never lonely while he had company, the singing of the birds; he even heard the red grouse calling from the heather. He mentioned the summer again. It was then that the weather was at its finest, brightest and sunniest. The plains were rich and fertile, the meadows wild and flowery and life was not difficult at all. There were beautiful sounds all around him, the wind making music in the woods; when the sky was grey overhead, river falls pouring over rocks and stones. 'Wonderful are the pines which make music for me, unasked for. I am no worse off than you are.'

Though Guaire enjoyed his kingship and the good things that went with it, Marbhan had that which went beyond all wealth – peace, tranquillity and contentment of spirit. He knew nothing of strife or combat, such as Guaire sometimes did. Rather he had every good thing in his little hut, his view of the world framed by its doorposts of heather and its lintel of honeysuckle. Guaire was so impressed with his brother's descriptions of nature that he would give all his great kingdom and everything in it to go and live with him.

There were other lovers of nature, among them the poet who penned these words in praise of the blackbird in the ninth century:

> The bird which calls from the willow.
> Beautiful beak of bright notes;
> musical yellow bill of a bright black lad;
> Fluted the tune that he plays for me, the blackbird's flute.

The poem 'The Scribe in the Woods' similarly celebrates the blackbird, but also has praise for the cuckoo:

> The clear voiced cuckoo calls to me,
> wonderful calling in grey feathers from the bushy tree tops.
> The Lord is indeed good to me;
> Well do I write under the trees.

Even St Colmcille longed to be back in Ireland

again, to hear the tuneful music of the swans on
Lough Foyle, while the seagulls gathering would
rejoice in the swiftness of his little boat. The sound
of the wind in the elms would make music for him
in the wild green woods, where the blackbirds'
startled cry would fill the summer's day.

Suibhne Geilt

Suibhne Geilt was King of the Dal nAraidhne in the ninth century, who was sometimes described as a historical figure, and other times a mythical one. According to the experts, however, Suibhne is not listed in the genealogies of the Dan nAraidhne, who held sway in parts of Antrim and Down, his story simply being a variant of a similar English tradition.

Suibhne sided with Congal Caoch, King of Ulaid, against the High King Domhnall Mac Aodha. According to tradition, Congal was stung by a bee in Domhnall's orchard, hence his epithet 'caoch' meaning one eyed. When the Ulaid demanded an eye from Domnall's son in reparation, however, the king would not agree, suggesting instead the destruction of the swarm so that at least the guilty bee would perish with the innocent. There was also tension between Domhnall and Congal at a feast at Tara, after which the battle of Mag Rath ensued in the year 637. It was in this battle that Suibhne supported Congal, having already had a confrontation with St Ronan, the latter cursing him for his attempts to expel the clerics from his kingdom. Suibhne's entry into the battle is described:

> The standard of Suibhne, a yellow banner,
> the renowned king of the Dal nAraidhne,
> Yellow satin over the mild man of hosts,
> the white fingered stipling himself in the middle of them.

Suibhne, however, was driven mad by the horrors of battle and fled from the place, deranged. It was said of him that he was filled with drunken terror and fear, that his entire body was converted into a confused, shaking mass. He leapt high in the air and flying like a bird landed on top of a yew tree. Not even the victorious High King himself was able to persuade him to come to his senses.

It was from then on that Suibhne made his
home in the wild and desolate places. He loved
the belling of the stag and praised the beauty of
the trees, extolling their virtues one by one: the
oak was high and leafy; the little hazel a treasure
trove of nuts; the alder friendly and kind; the
blackthorn thorny but the bearer of sloes; the
rowan tree had beautiful blossoms and berries;
the sheltering holly a barrier against the wind; the
ash tree useful for making weapons; the birch tree
beautiful in every single branch, the leaves of the
poplar shaking like a stream.

He remembered with regret his confrontation
with the saint, 'Under bad omens did I sully
the good name of Ronan Finn; his miracles and
monastery bell have brought me trouble.' It was
his misfortune too that he had chosen to side with
Congal, the latter's tunic wonderfully decorated
and trimmed with gold. He remembered flying
over the ivied trees of the woods to escape the
horrors of battle, to escape the weapons of
the enemy too. He listed many of the places
he had been, but sometimes went home to
Glenn mBolcain, reputedly the place where the
madmen of Ireland congregated, and where
they lived on watercress and berries. It had its

counterpart, Gleann na nGealt (the glen of the mad men) in Co. Kerry. Suibhne loved the wild, and the wilderness of Glenn mBolcain. Even if he were to wander all over the world, he would prefer a little hut of his own in the glen. He loved everything about it, its crystal streams, its wild green watercress. His friend and relative came to him, disguised as a mill-hag, bringing him the baleful news that his father and mother, son and daughter were all dead. It was news which wounded him, Suibhne said, and he wished he had not stayed to hear it. He described the proud ivy twined round the twisted trees, as he sallied forth before the larks. He could even overtake the beautiful wood pigeons, because strangely he too had grown feathers. Woodcocks fluttered before him, blackbirds gave cries of alarm and little foxes had feasts of their own. Sometimes the foxes ran to him, sometimes they ran from him.

He feared the coming of the starry frosts in winter for then he would be exposed to the cold on the high mountain peaks. He loved the herons and the blackbirds and the sound of badgers calling. All of these were far more musical to him than the sounds of men. He listed the stags one by one and gave the names of their high mountain homes, again illustrating the old Irish love of place-lore. One time he caught sight of a stag looking towards the glen and mused to himself that the top of the antlers would be a very good place for a lookout, 'I am wandering Suibhne; swiftly I run across the heathery glens.' He loved the clear water of the wells, wells unrivalled in Ireland, and the fronds of the bracken turning russet and red all around him.

The extent of Suibhne's wanderings is

mentioned time and time again. He mentions the Mourne mountains in Co. Down for instance, and the Stacks mountains in Kerry at the other end of the country:

> I have been troubled by frost, the most inclement of weather. The snow has swirled around me on the Kerry Stacks; far from me the heather of lovely Glenn mBolchain. Restless my wandering from place to place.

There is a kind of pathos in his description of his loneliness, 'falling from the limbs of withered branches, running through furze, something I have done; shunning mankind to be wolves and racing stags'. He loved the sound of the roaring river when it seemed to rush against the first waves of the sea:

> I hear melodies in it, in the time of its winter might. I sleep to the sound of its harmonies on the cold and starry night. I hear the tuneful birds of the shore: lovely their cries and lonely in the moonlit air.

It was St Ronan's curse that had brought Suibhne

into the company of the wild. All of his adventures are in fact described in the romance called *Buile Suibhne*. In the end, it was with St Moling that he was finally reconciled with the Church, the saint giving him the last sacraments before he died.

The Poetry of Nature

The world of nature inspired some of the richest poetry and prose of ancient Ireland. It was a time when awareness of nature was at its most powerful and expressive, influencing as it did almost every aspect of daily life. The tale of Cano, son of Gartnan is essentially the story of a Pictish prince in exile in Ireland. Gartnan and his rival were in contention for the kingship of Scotland. Gartnan lived on the island of Innis Moccu Chein, where it was said of him that he had fifty nets for wild game and fifty fishing nets fitted with bells. A bell rang at the windows of the kitchen every time a salmon was caught, while Gartnan himself drank mead on his quilted bed.

Gartnan hid a great vat of gold on the shore at low tide but when he was killed by his rival Aodhan, his son Cano fled to Ireland, where he was welcomed by the joint kings Dairmait and Blathmac. Aodhan, with the aid of evil forces, found the hidden treasure and used it to try and bribe the kings to have Cano slain, but Cano was warned in time. 'They are counting out the gold for your murder in that room there', the daughter of Diarmait told him. When he confronted them, however, the kings assured him that he would not be betrayed at all. In a hunting scene soon after, Cano and his men journeyed across Muirthime into Mag Brega at a place called Cernae. There were swans on the slope there but when Cano made a cast at them, he missed and instantly regretted his actions, 'I have frightened the swans of Cernae. Now I wish I had not thrown at all. They are sad at being disturbed, just as I am for throwing the stone.' The next day, his company urged him to make another cast at the birds but he vowed never to do so again. It was not to make war on the swans that he set out from Skye and travelled the seas to Ireland.

He travelled to Connaught where he fell in love with Creidh, the daughter of King Guaire, promising to return to her when he had won the kingship of Scotland. He left her a magic stone, a fairy stone given to his mother by two women of the sidhe when she lay in childbirth. He eventually won the kingship but his love with Creidh was not to be.

Liadin was a poetess of the seventh century, who according to tradition belonged to the people of Corca Dhuibhne in Co. Kerry. When she went to Connaught she fell in love with the handsome Cuirithir Mac Dobharcon, his surname literally meaning 'son of the otter'. She did not stay with Cuirithir, however, but when he came looking for her she went with him. Cuirithir, however, was sent away by Cumaine, a saint of the period, and becoming a monk, he settled in the lands of the Deise in Co. Wexford. It was there that Liadin followed him, but by the time she arrived, he had already sailed away in his currach, leaving Liadin to pine on the flagstone where he used to pray. 'I am Liadin. I loved Cuirithir', she said, 'This is as true as anything ever told. The music of the woods sang to us, when we were together; we loved the singing of the sea.' Then, giving herself up to sadness, she died of a broken heart.

Deirdre too lamented the death of her lover Naoise in *The Exile of the Sons of Uisneach*:

> Dear his soft grey eyes that women loved;
> fierce to his foes they were;
> After a circuit of the forest in the morning, a beautiful place.
> Dear his voice in the wild green wood.

Sorrow, she said, was stronger than the sea, and if

King Conchobar were wise, he would surely know
this.

The nature of poetry of the period was vivid
and sensual, filled as it was with colour and sound
and imagining. Of Mongan the shape changer it
was said:

> He will be an antlered stag in the lands where
> chariots are driven;
> he will be a speckled salmon in a bright pool;
> he will be a seal and a swan, a graceful swan drifting
> on the tide.

The poems celebrated the earth and the seasons
and the beauty of the world around us. They
painted wonderful pictures of autumn, when the
dappled fawns followed in the wake of the hinds
and were nurtured in the purple heather. It is
this emphasis on colour that adds to the lyricism
of the poems themselves. The stags made noise
on the hills but there was peace and quiet in the
woods. The fields of grain flourished far and wide
and the good earth was full of ripening fruits.
Winter, however was bleaker by far. Then a flood
of waves crashed against the shores of earth and
the seabirds cried in the wind. Spring, however,

stirred the birds from the islands, the animals from the woods and the green grass grew again. Summer was the most wonderful of all. The leaves were resplendent then, green the colour of the sheltering grove; the shining streams dried up, good tidings in the sight of fine dry turf. It was essentially a celebration of nature in all its richness and diversity.

The story of Diarmuid and Gráinne is one of the best known of all Irish stories and not surprisingly it too has inspired the poets:

'O where is Gráinne, the golden, the beautiful?
And like the flowing of sea waves others cried:
O where is Gráinne, the golden, that was wed,
Yet was not wife?' And a sad voice replied
'Lo Gráinne, the golden, the beautiful is dead
And her red lips are dust.' The warriors sighed
Bowed as if sank in sleep. Arose
Gráinne, the sweet voiced, spake out laughingly,
'O men. Ye pale as poplars when wind blows rainly
Ye drowse and grow afraid of dreams.'

Epilogue

There is one story which perhaps more than and other illustrates the old Irish love of nature. When the King Feradach Fechtnach died, his two sons Tuathal and Fiacha made a division of Ireland between them. One of them took the country's wealth and her treasure, her castles, her seated dwellings and her fortresses, the other her cliffs and her estuaries, her fruits and her fishes, her salmon and her game. When Caoilte told his story to the nobles of Christian Ireland, they protested, saying the division was unfair. The former son had been given the better bargain of it, for if they themselves had been given the choice, they would have opted for 'her wealth and her treasures and all her good things'. Caoilte had other ideas, however, 'That part which you deem the worse is the one that we would have chosen: her rivers, her wastes, her wilds and her woods, her sea cliffs and estuaries too.' According to the story, it was the younger son, Fiacha who chose these things and who subsequently joined the Fianna. On the death of his brother, however, he assumed the kingship. The story illustrates the regard in which nature was held by Caoilte and the Fianna, and all of those who peopled the myths of long ago.